E. Wagner

FOUNDATION
TO
FLUTE PLAYING

AN ELEMENTARY METHOD

CARL FISCHER®
62 Cooper Square, New York, NY 10003

Copyright © 1918 by Carl Fischer, Inc., New York
Copyright renewed
International Copyright Secured

0 8258 0054 4

CONTENTS

THEOBALD BOEHM

THEOBALD BOEHM was born in Munich, Germany, on April 9th, 1794. In his youth he was quite delicate, but through the lung exercise which he derived from playing the flute, he eventually became possessed of unusual strength. Being of a mechanical as well as an artistic frame of mind, he realized in his early youth that the flute was a very imperfect instrument, and he devoted most of his time to its improvement. At sixteen years of age, he made a flute for his own use, and at eighteen he held the position of first flutist at a theatre in Munich. In about 1828, Boehm established a factory for the manufacture of flutes. These instruments were still of the old style, but their mechanism was considerably improved. After almost twenty years of toil and study, the new system instrument, universally known as the Boehm Flute, was given to the world in 1847.

Theobald Boehm's name will always be a household word among flutists. He died in 1881 at the age of eighty-seven years.

INTRODUCTION

In writing this book, my idea was simply to provide a method for beginners, which would progress systematically by slow degrees, thus giving the student an opportunity of acquiring a solid foundation. There are many wonderful flute methods published, some of which go too far beyond the capabilities of the student, after the first few pages. I have tried to make this book precisely what its name implies— a Foundation, pure and simple.

The exercises are explained in detail, and the student who is not within reach of a competent teacher, should find this work easy to comprehend. I have tried to write the lessons as though I were giving them personally to each student. Every effort has been made to make the exercises pleasing and melodious, so as to increase the student's interest with each lesson.

Those who have mastered these exercises, and have profited by the advice and suggestions given, will have a good foundation upon which to build, and there is no reason why they should not become excellent players. This book should serve as a fine preparation for the other standard and more advanced methods.

If this work will start flutists on the proper path, I will be happy in the thought that its mission has been accomplished.

ERNEST F. WAGNER

POSITION

When practicing, always stand, if at all possible.

Stand erect and expand the chest.

Keep the right elbow higher than the left. The left elbow should not be too close to the body. The position should be free and comfortable.

Stand before a mirror when practicing, in order to correct any faulty position.

Avoid any contortions of the face. A normal condition is to be desired.

The cheeks should not be puffed out. This is a very common fault, and one which adds nothing to the ease of playing.

The player who puffs out his cheeks loses the muscular control of his lips, and his articulation will become impaired.

Do not lift the fingers too high or keep them too stiff. Let them bend naturally over the keys.

The thumb of the right hand should always be kept in the same place, viz., under the first and second fingers.

Endeavor to secure a position of perfect repose.

THE FLUTE

Adjustment and Care

The flute consists of three parts; the head-joint, the middle-joint, and the tail- or foot-joint. On the head-joint there are no keys, but at the upper end is the blow-hole, or embouchure, through which the sound is produced. On the middle- and tail-joints are the keys by which the instrument is played.

To put the flute together properly, place the upper end of the middle-joint between the thumb and forefinger of the left hand, take the tail-piece by its lower end, and, with a gentle turn, slide the tail-joint on to the lower cork end of the middle-joint to the position in which the little finger of the right hand will fall directly on the D♯ key. To adjust the head-joint, retain the same position of the middle-joint in the hollow of the thumb of the left hand, and with the right hand gently turn the head-joint into the position where the blow-hole or embouchure is in a direct line with the keys of the middle-joint. The exact position of the blow-hole cannot be uniform, but must be determined by the individual. Some can produce a better tone by having it slightly turned out, others by having it slightly turned in. This is caused by the different formations of the lips, and the position of the head while playing.

Take the flute apart the same way it was put together. After playing, dry out each joint with a soft piece of silk wrapped around a thin cleaning stick, which comes with the purchase of most flutes. To keep the keys bright, wipe the perspiration from them with the piece of silk before putting the instrument away.

For hygienic reasons, never allow anyone to use your flute.

The bearings and delicate parts of your instrument cannot work well forever without attention now and then. A little oil should be used frequently.

It is not essential to pull out the stopper which is located in the head-joint each time the instrument is wiped, but if you are accustomed to doing it, be careful that it is properly replaced.

The stopper in the head-joint should not be tampered with. It will be found in its proper place if the first, second and third D can be produced in perfect tune.

It is best to have a mark on the projecting end of the cork-screw, that one may always place the cork exactly at the correct distance, 17 millimeters (about 11-16 of an inch) from the center of the blow-hole.

How to Practice

Set aside a regular time for practice each day if possible.

Do not attempt too much at first, and do not get discouraged if the first lessons prove tiresome and monotonous.

In striking tones, especially in rapid execution, the fingers and the tongue must work simultaneously.

Play all music exactly as written.

Practice in such a manner that you can play without apparent effort, and can derive pleasure from it.

Do not practice too long at one time. Too much or too strenuous practice is as harmful as too little. Use discretion. Always cease practicing when the lips begin to grow tired. Do not try to practice for an hour or more at a stretch. It is often an impossibility, and always does more harm than good. When the lips are in good condition, do not tire or strain them. Rest every little while. Playing when the lips are tired weakens them, and is to be avoided whenever possible. Fifteen minutes of correct practice is more beneficial than four hours of carelessness.

Do not spend too much time on high tones; too much of this sort of practice weakens the lips materially.

What to Practice

Practice whatever may be necessary and what you are not familiar with. Do not neglect the remote keys.

Practice sustained tones for ten or fifteen minutes each day. This strengthens the lips, and greatly improves the quality of tone. Nothing in the way of practice is more important.

Do not sacrifice tone for technique. A good tone is a performer's most valuable asset.

Do not fail to practice all sorts of exercises and scales, and do not give up until they are completely mastered.

Give particular attention to quality of tone, also to style of performance and to phrasing.

Avoid the "tremolo" or "vibrato" style of playing. See that your tone is absolutely clear and pure.

Transposition

Learn to transpose. This is a positive necessity for professionals, and is very convenient and desirable for amateurs. It should not be studied, however, until the pupil has a fair knowledge of the rudiments of music, and is beyond the first stages of playing.

Fingering

The fingerings given in this method are exactly as they were given to the writer by the late Carl Wehner, who was a pupil of Boehm himself. There are many methods which give different fingerings for the quick passages, such as taking the F♯ in the first space and on the fifth line with the middle finger of the right hand, and the high F♯ with the third finger of the right hand, also the use of the double B♭ Key in playing in flat keys.

I have always found it expedient to teach the correct fingering at first, in order to develop all the fingers. After one is able to play fairly well, he will soon discover which is the easiest and simplest way to play certain passages.

The Crutch (or Bridge)

The use of the crutch is a matter of personal taste. Most players of the closed G♯ flute do not use it, while almost all who play the open G♯ flute find that it has its advantages, especially when playing in the upper register. It is usually well for beginners to use the crutch, as it affords a certain support for the left hand.

Open and Closed G♯ Key

There has always been more or less controversy regarding the merits of the open and closed G♯ key. The flute with the closed G♯ key was first made to enable the players of the old or Meyer system flute to change over to the Boehm system without altering the fingering for the G♯, as all the old flutes were made with the closed G♯ key.

Boehm, in his book, "The Flute and Flute Playing," gives many reasons for his preference for the open G♯ flute, the principal one being that all the fingers of the left hand are used for closing the keys, while on the closed G♯ flute, the little finger is used to open the G♯ key, causing a contrary motion for that finger. Another reason is that, scientifically, the open G♯ flute is more perfect.

The high E♮ on the closed G♯ flute is usually thin in quality and inclined to be somewhat too sharp in pitch. The writer prefers the open G♯ flute. However, there are more closed G♯ flutes in use than the other, and some of the most prominent players use them for one reason or another.

Whether the student plays the open or the closed G♯ flute, it matters not as far as the music for the instrument is concerned. All the music in this book can be used to advantage on instruments of either system. The charts give the fingering for both flutes, and the student should study the fingering very conscientiously.

Breathing

Breathe through the mouth. Take breath according to the length of phrase to be played.

Do not try to play as much as possible on one breath.

Tuning

A small breath will sustain quite a long phrase, so do not inhale more breath than is needed.

Never start to play together with some other instrument or instruments before tuning carefully.

No wind instruments, whether reed or brass, are perfectly in tune; but they can be regulated, and the bad places humored, if the performer has a good ear and a fairly strong lip.

Train your ear and you will have little difficulty in playing well in tune.

The embouchure is not always the same, and the head-joint must be drawn accordingly.

Heat and cold have opposite effects on the instrument. When the flute is cold, it is flat; when warm, it is sharp.

Time

Always bear in mind that rhythm is the most important factor in music.

To play in perfect rhythm it is essential to give all notes their proper time-value.

Without rhythm, there is no music.

Practice your exercises slowly at first, in order to play the correct notes. After you have mastered the notes, begin to play in the proper tempo, which is generally indicated by some suitable Italian word.

Do not count or keep time by moving the body or the feet. That is a very bad habit.

Counting must be done mentally.

You must think as you play.

Before Playing

Be sure that the instrument is in perfect condition before commencing to play.

Always be sure of the key in which you are to play. Remember that there is a vast difference between F and G, for example, especially in the fingering.

Always see that the instrument is properly tuned to the pitch of the piano, violin or other instrument which is to be used at the same time.

Before starting to play, always look the music over well and figure out how you are going to count and divide the beats.

Do not play directly after eating a heavy meal. Give the food time to digest.

General Preliminary Advice

No lesson in this work will be quite as important as the first, and it is on just such fundamental exercises as these that the student often spends too little time. It is a serious mistake to try to build the foundation too quickly. Each individual exercise should be well within one's grasp before the next one is attempted. It is not to be expected that the student will be able to control his tones immediately at the start. Some players acquire the "knack" of striking the tones very quickly, others take longer, but in the end may get it just as well. It is not necessary for the student to learn an entire lesson each day. Take plenty of time and get one exercise perfect before the next is attempted.

If one learns to attack his notes and to sustain them properly at the start, he will have little or no trouble in the future, provided he continues his studies systematically and conscientiously. Keep the lips closed as much as possible at all times. Raise the flute to the lips, not directly to the blow-hole but a few inches below, draw it to the right until the lips are in position, and be careful not to cover more than half of the blow-hole. Do not feel around with the tongue for the blow-hole as it is an unnecessary and unsightly habit. With a little practice in drawing the flute in position as explained above, you will soon acquire a perfect position.

Keep the lips closed and pronounce the syllable "Tu" as you would in the word *tune*, and the lips will voluntarily open sufficiently to produce the sound. Be sure there is enough tension at the corners of the mouth to keep control of the tone. Opening the lips too far will mean loss of control and cause the tone to drop in pitch and become flat.

After you have learned to produce the first note, C, look in a mirror and see that all fingers of both hands are in their proper position. Play it over and over again until you get it well under control and can play it with a clear tone.

Additional Advice

Above all, secure a good instrument and a competent instructor. Although perhaps a trifle more expensive at the outset, it will prove much more economical in the end.

If you have not a musical dictionary, you should secure one. It is a real necessity.

Ensemble playing—duos, trios, orchestra and band practice—is exceedingly beneficial, and should be indulged in whenever possible.

Orchestra playing is generally better for the student than band, as the latter is apt to be too strenuous, and tone quality is sacrificed for power.

Hear good music, especially when rendered by eminent performers on different instruments. Embrace every opportunity of hearing great singers, and imitate their style of performance as much as possible.

Aim for the highest in music—do not be satisfied with anything mediocre.

By conscientious practice, the student will ultimately master all difficulties.

Advancement can only be made by careful study and practice.

It is not good to attempt too much at one time.

Nothing is too easy to practice.

It benefits even advanced players to play the simplest kinds of exercises.

All kinds of exercises are beneficial.

Rudiments of Music

Music is the art of combining sounds in a manner agreeable to the ear.

It is divided into two parts: Melody and Harmony.

Melody is a combination of sounds which, by their elevation, duration and succession, serve to form a tune.

Harmony is another combination of sounds which, by their simultaneous union, serve to form chords.

The Signs used to represent sound are called Notes.

The five lines upon which notes are written are called the Staff.

The Staff consists of five lines and four spaces.

Extra lines are used above and below the staff. They are called Ledger Lines.

Seven letters of the alphabet are used to designate the notes; they are C - D - E - F - G - A - B.

At the beginning of each line of music you will find the Clef Sign ()

The Clef is used to determine the position and pitch of the scale. This clef is called the G or Treble Clef. It shows where G is, thereby giving place to the other notes. The sign crosses the second line "G" four times.

There are other clefs, but they are not used in Flute music.

There are seven natural tones in music, to which is added an eighth tone, which however, is only a repetition of the first tone an octave higher.

When the notes are written in the Treble Clef, the names of the lines and spaces are as follows:——

LINES

SPACES

The notes that can be written on the staff are not enough to enable us to indicate all the tones that are within the range and compass of the Flute. For this reason, it becomes necessary to go beyond the staff, and use what are termed "Ledger Lines and Spaces."

LEDGER NOTES

The distance between two notes is called "interval".

NOTES

There are seven characters which determine the value of notes.

- **o**   whole note — 4 beats or counts.
- **♩**   half note — 2 beats or counts.
- **♩**   quarter note — 1 beat or count.
- **♪**   eighth note — $\frac{1}{2}$ beat.
- **♫**   sixteenth note —
- **♬**   thirty-second note —
- **♬**   sixty-fourth note —

RESTS

There are seven characters that denote the value of rests.

- **▬**   whole rest — 4 beats or counts.
- **▬**   half rest — 2 beats or counts.
- **𝄽**   quarter rest — 1 beat or count.
- **𝄾**   eighth rest — $\frac{1}{2}$ beat or count
- **𝄿**   sixteenth rest —
- **𝅀**   thirty-second rest —
- **𝅁**   sixty-fourth rest —

A Rest is a character used to indicate silence, or a temporary suspension of sounds.

SHARPS, FLATS, NATURALS ETC.

The Sharp (♯) raises the note half a tone.

The Flat (♭) lowers the note half a tone.

The Natural (♮) restores the note which has been changed by the ♯ or ♭ to its former position.

The Double Sharp (✕) raises a note a half tone higher than the simple (♯) would raise it. In other words, it raises the note a whole tone.

The Double Flat (♭♭) sinks a note a half tone lower than the simple (♭) would lower it, — in other words, a whole tone.

Always after the Clef, we must look for the Signature, or key, in which we are to play.

The word Signature signifies a certain number of sharps or flats placed immediately after the clef.

Either sharps or flats found after the Clef as Signature, influence the notes placed on the same degree, or at the upper or lower octave, during the whole of a piece of music, unless a natural comes accidentally to suspend their effect.

If a sharp or flat is written in any bar without being designated at the beginning (in the Signature), such sharp or flat is called an "Accidental", and holds good only for the bar in which it is written. If this sign is to be contradicted, in said bar, a "natural" must be placed before the note in question.

MEASURES AND BARS

Musical Composition is divided into equal portions,— called Measures or Bars, by short lines drawn across the staff which are also called Bars.

A double Bar is placed at the end of each strain of music.

Measures are divided into equal parts called "beats".

All music does not begin with a perfect or full bar. The first bar may be imperfect and contain what is known as "start notes". There may be one or more of such start notes. However, the first and last bars of a strain, or of a complete piece, must together form a full bar.

TIME MARKS

Immediately after the signature comes the Time Mark.

There are various kinds of time marks, but those most frequently used are, 4/4 - 3/4 - 2/4 and 6/8.

There are many other time marks, such as, 2/2 - 3/2 - 6/4 - 5/4 - 3/8 - 9/8 - 12/8, etc., etc., but in this book, only the simpler forms will be used.

The upper figure (numerator) indicates the number of notes of a given kind in the measure.

The lower figure (denominator) shows the kind of notes, taken as the unit of measure.

Time refers to the number of beats to the measure.

Tempo indicates the rapidity of the beats.

The two are often confounded.

• A Dot placed after a note or rest prolongs its value by half. ♩. would be the same as ♩♪ A second or third dot prolongs the time value of the dot immediately preceding it by half. ♩... would be the same as ♩♩♪♪

— *Tenuto.* This line when placed over or under a note signifies that the tone should be well sustained, for its full value.

⌢ or ⌣ *Hold* or *Pause,* placed over or under a note or rest indicates an indefinite prolongation of its time value, at the performer's discretion.

⫴ *Repeat.* This sign signifies that the division between the dotted double bars is to be repeated.

𝄒 *Breathing mark.* A sign which indicates where breath may be taken.

⌒ *Slur* or *Tie.* This sign indicates that when two or more notes are joined by it, they are to be played in a smooth and connected manner (Legato). If the notes so joined are on the same degree of the staff, they are held over as one note.

< *Crescendo,* increasing in loudness, by degrees.

> *Decrescendo,* growing softer by degrees.

∧ *Sforzato,* marked or sudden emphasis.

⌇ *tr Trill,* the rapid alternation of a principal note with a higher auxiliary, (major or minor second above).

∾ *Turn* or *Grupetto,* a melodic grace consisting in what may be termed the typical form (the direct turn), of four notes, a principal note (twice struck) with its higher and lower auxiliary (the major and minor second above and below, each struck once.)

M.M. ♩=60 *Metronome mark,* a mark often set at the beginning of a composition for exactly indicating its tempo. The ♩=60 means, that the time value of one quarter note is equal to one pendulum-beat with the slider set at 60. With the slider set at 60, the pendulum makes one beat per second. M. M. actually stands for "Maelzel's Metronome," named after its inventor, Maelzel, of Vienna. The Metronome is much used by beginners and students, for learning to play strictly in time and in timing their practice.

f — *Forte,* means loud, strong.

ff — *Fortissimo,* means very loud.

mf — *Mezzo-forte,* half loud.

p — *Piano,* soft.

pp — *Pianissimo,* very soft.

D.C. — *Da Capo,* from the beginning.

D.S. — *Dal Segno,* repeat from the sign.

———— ◆ ————

For other signs etc., see Coon's Standard Pocket Dictionary of Musical Terms.

1st Lesson
ATTACK

Keep D♯ key open with little finger of right hand for all exercises on this page.

1. All keys open except first key marked 1 for first finger, left hand.

2. Close single B key with thumb of left hand. It is usually found to left on open G♯ flute, to the right on closed G♯ flute.

3. Leaving first finger and thumb down, close key marked 2 with second finger of left hand.

4. Leaving down the fingers that are already down, close keys marked 3 and 4 with third and fourth fingers of left hand on open G♯ flute, and only key marked 3 with third finger on closed G♯ flute.

5. While counting measure rest, take fingering for next note. Always be sure position is correct. Faulty position and bad habits are easily acquired at first and difficult to remedy later.

6. This exercise includes all notes previously practiced.

7. From G to C, ascending and descending.

8. This exercise is a trifle more difficult because the notes are in a different rotation. Always think ahead for the fingering of the next note.

2nd Lesson
ATTACK

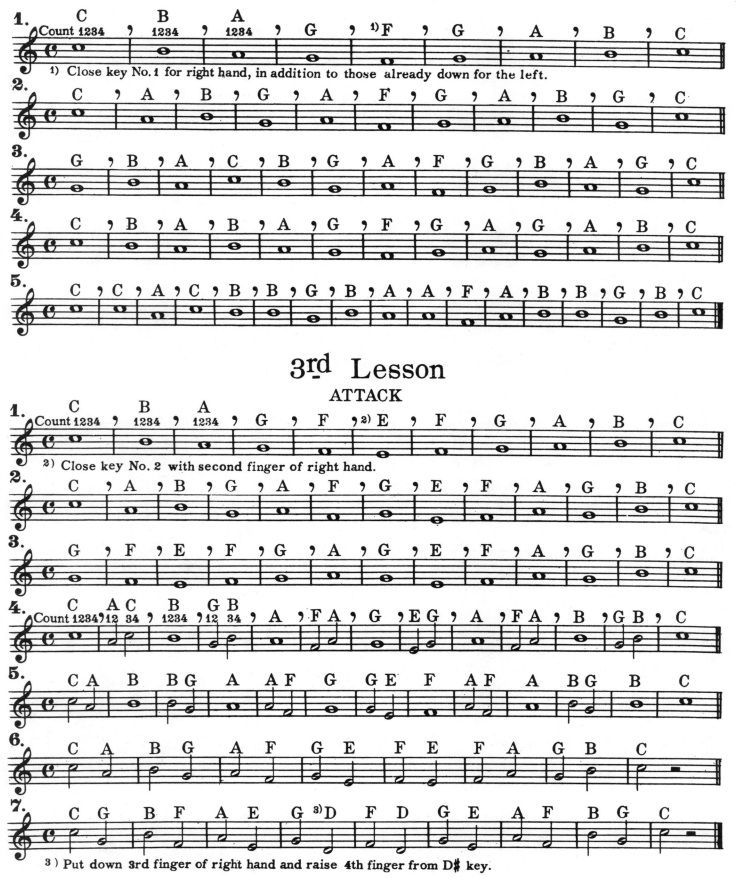

1) Close key No. 1 for right hand, in addition to those already down for the left.

2) Close key No. 2 with second finger of right hand.

3rd Lesson
ATTACK

3) Put down 3rd finger of right hand and raise 4th finger from D♯ key.

4th Lesson
ATTACK

1.

C   , D , C , D , C , D , C , D , C

This exercise introduces D in the second register. Close all keys that are open for C and raise fingers that are down for D. D♯ key always open for C, but closed for D.

2.

C   D   E   D   C   E   D   C   D   E   C

This exercise introduces E in the second register. Same fingering as low E. Slightly more lip pressure from now on.

3.

C   D   E   F   E   D   F   E   D   C

This exercise introduces F in the second register. Same fingering as low F.

4.

C   D   E   F   G   F   E   D   F   E   G   F   E   D   C

This exercise introduces G in the second register. Same fingering as low G.

5.

These exercises in half notes include all notes previously practiced.

6.

7. Whole and half notes.

8.

9.

This exercise is somewhat longer. Do not tire the lips — rest when necessary.

5th Lesson
ATTACK

1. Scale of G

Refer to p. 9, "Sharps, Flats, Naturals, etc.," and consult chart for fingering of F♯.

2. Arpeggio of G

3. Whole notes, half notes and half rests

4. Quarter notes
Count 1 2 3 4   12   34   1 2 3 4   12   34

5.

Attention to intonation of E, which is inclined to be a trifle flat on Boehm flutes.

6. Scale exercise

7.

Full value to rests.

8.

Intervals of the third between first and second notes of meas. 1 – 6.

6th Lesson

ATTACK

1. Scale of C, range two octaves

Low C with all fingers down, fourth finger of right hand on C and C# keys instead of D# key.

2. Arpeggio of C, range two octaves

3. Scale exercise

4. Scale exercise, upper octave

5. Triple rhythm

Introducing method of counting eighth notes

6. Count 1 2 and 3 4 and

Play staccato and very evenly

7.

BLUE BELLS OF SCOTLAND

8.

7th Lesson

ATTACK

1. Scale of D

2. Arpeggio of D

3. Quadruple rhythm
Count 1 2 3 4

4. Triple rhythm
Count 1 2 3 1 2 3 1 2 3

5. Eighths and quarters in triple rhythm
Count 1 2 3 1 2 3

6. Quarters, eighths and dotted halves
Count 1 2 3 4

7. Quarters and eighths in duple rhythm
Count 1 2 1 2

8th Lesson

CONSTRUCTION OF SCALES

INTRODUCTORY

A scale consists of eight consecutive notes (technically called degrees, counting from any note to its octave) separated by intervals of whole-tones (major seconds) and half-tones (minor seconds).

Counting upward in the major scales the half-tones are between the 3rd and 4th and the 7th and 8th degrees of the scale.

There are twenty-four scales in common use, one major and one minor for each of the twelve divisions of the octave. Of the seven intervals in each scale two are half-tones and the rest are whole-tones.

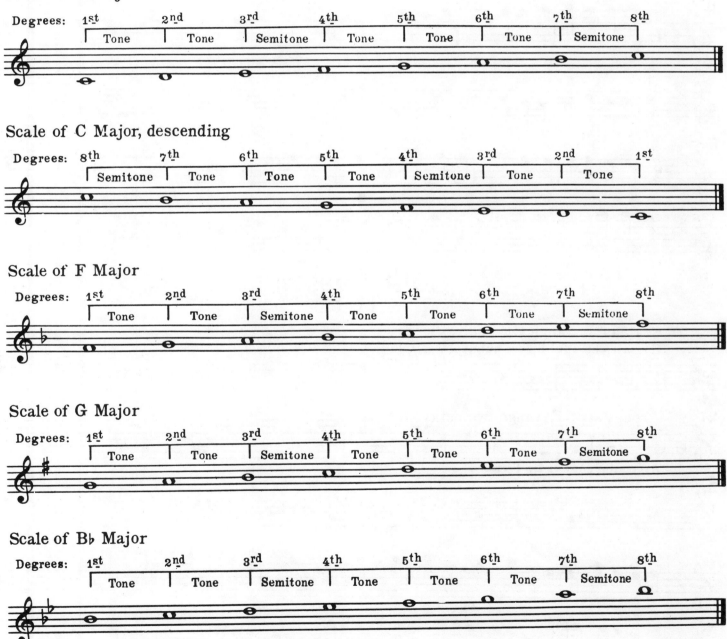

9th Lesson
ATTACK

Scale of D, range two octaves
1. For higher notes, less opening of lips, and slightly more pressure at corners of mouth.

2. **Arpeggio of D, range two octaves**

3. Attention to change of fingering from C# to D.

4.

5.

10th Lesson
ATTACK

1. **Scale of F, range two octaves**
Consult chart for higher notes.

2. **Arpeggio of F, range two octaves**
(Ascending, lower lip forward)

3.

4.

11th Lesson
DOTTED QUARTER NOTES FOLLOWED BY EIGHTHS

This is a rhythmic figure that is often incorrectly played. Since the dot increases the value of a note by half, the dotted quarter has the value of a quarter plus an eighth. Therefore it takes a count and a half; the following eighth occupies the other half count.

12th Lesson
THE SLUR[1]

1. Minor seconds in C (All the intervals will be found in the 51st lesson.)

When slurring to a higher note, contract lips.

When slurring to a lower note, relax lips.

2. Seconds in C

3. Thirds in C

4. Thirds in G

5. Fourths in F

6. Study in D

[1] First note is struck with the tongue (attacked) and connected with all other notes under or over the same slur. This style of playing is called *legato*.

13th Lesson
THE SLUR
(Varied articulations)

14th Lesson

SIMPLE TONGUING EXERCISES

These exercises are to be played very staccato in strict time, always attacking each unslurred note separately. Practice slowly at first, then gradually increase the speed.

15th Lesson

SLURRING AND TONGUING
(Varied Articulations)

1. Pronounce the syllable "tu" very distinctly.

2.

3. Large commas show breathing places.

4. O COME ALL YE FAITHFUL

5.

16th Lesson
MISCELLANEOUS SLURRING EXERCISES

1. Count

First count 6 in a measure, then increase the speed and count 2 in a measure, playing 3 notes to each count.

2. Count 1 2 3 4

In measure 7 open the D♯ key with 4th finger of right hand for every note except D.

3. Count 1 2

4. Count 1 2

Finger D♭ same as C♯. (Meas. 9)

17th Lesson

SYNCOPATION

Syncopation occurs when the usual accent is displaced. It results from tying unaccented notes to accented notes, or from placing long notes between short ones in a single measure.

18th Lesson
STACCATO TONGUING

1. Practice slowly at first.

19th Lesson
STACCATO EXERCISES IN 6/8 TIME

20th Lesson
MISCELLANEOUS EXERCISES
(in G Major)

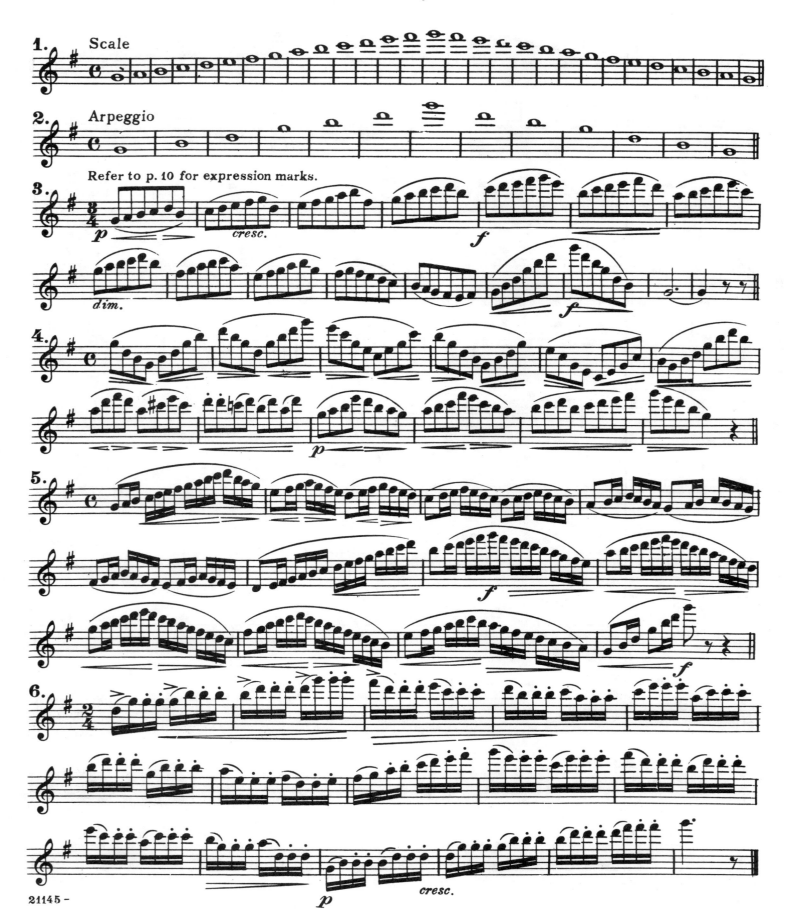

1. Scale

2. Arpeggio

Refer to p. 10 for expression marks.

3.

4.

5.

6.

21$\underline{^{st}}$ Lesson
MISCELLANEOUS EXERCISES
(in F Major)

Twenty-second Lesson

MISCELLANEOUS EXERCISES
(In D Major)

This lesson in D major will include the second and third octaves. The high B♮ in the third octave should not be too difficult for the pupil to master at this time. But since the fingering for the third octave is rather complicated, it will of necessity require more practice time to reach perfection. Look at the fingering chart to be absolutely sure the fingering is correct.

No. 1 is the D major scale up to the high B♮ in the third octave.

No. 2 is the chord of D major up to high A in all three octaves.

No. 3 is a short exercise in 4/4 or common time, which includes every note of the D major scale up to high G.

No. 4 is an exercise in 3/4 time, with sixteenth notes, which will be very beneficial if practiced slowly at first and gradually increasing the tempo.

No. 5 is a more difficult exercise in 2/4 time, sixteenth notes. If the scale and chord have been practiced sufficiently it should not be too difficult. The pupil should bear in mind that there is no short cut to perfection, which can only be acquired by diligent and intelligent study.

22nd Lesson
MISCELLANEOUS EXERCISES
(in D Major)

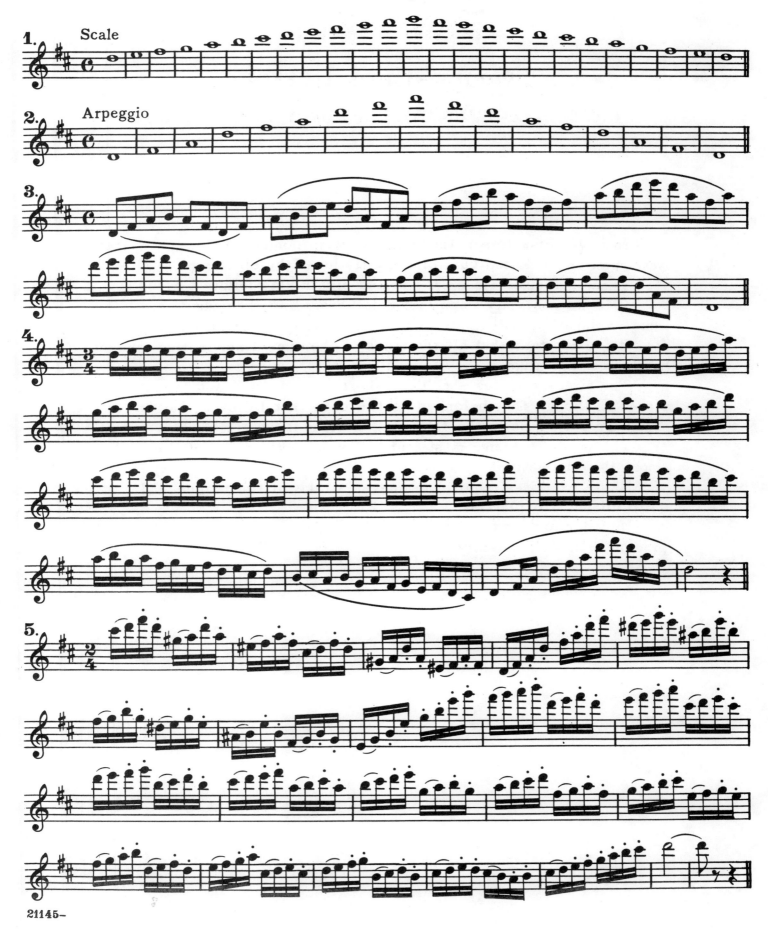

Twenty - third Lesson

DOTTED EIGHTHS FOLLOWED BY SIXTEENTHS

In a previous lesson, the exercises were similar to these, only they were written in dotted quarter notes followed by eighths.

These exercises are on the dotted eighth note followed by sixteenths.

It is not necessary to go into detail regarding each exercise, as the same explanation will apply to all.

It is important that all the notes of the same denomination should have the same value.

The sixteenth notes should be short and precise and should be played as though they belonged to the note that follows; that is, they should be pushed on to the following note, as it were.

This sort of exercise must sound very snappy and full of life. Play smoothly and lightly.

These exercises require an uneven stroke of the tongue and are quite difficult to play fast.

In order to play them so that they will sound well, much careful practice will be necessary.

23rd Lesson
DOTTED EIGHTHS FOLLOWED BY SIXTEENTHS

21145 –

Twenty-fourth Lesson
STACCATO EXERCISES IN SIXTEENTH NOTES

A good staccato is very necessary to flutists. Both single and double tonguing are used. Double tonguing will be dealt with later on. These exercises are all meant to be played with single tonguing.

No. 1 is in 2/4 time. Key of G Major. Should be played very short and snappy and with good rhythm.

No. 2 is in 3/4 time. Key of D Major. Count three beats to each bar. The eighth notes must be played short, but be careful and not hurry them. Keep perfect time, so that the last bar is no slower or faster than the first. A good plan is to play these exercises with a"Metronome", increasing the tempo gradually. In the fourth bar, G♯ occurs for the first time. Consult the chart for the correct fingering.

No. 3 is in 4/4 time. Key of F Major. The first four notes form the leading tones or up-beat. Notice that the rhythm is exactly opposite from exercise 1 in that the two sixteenths come ahead of the eighths in most instances.

No. 4 is in 2/4 time. Key of B♭ Major, and is perhaps the most difficult exercise in this lesson. It will be necessary to take breath very quickly so that the rhythm will not be broken, The tongue and fingers must move simultaneously.

24 th Lesson

STACCATO EXERCISES IN SIXTEENTH NOTES

25th Lesson

MISCELLANEOUS EXERCISES

(in B♭ Major)

Consult chart for fingering of high E♭ and B♭.

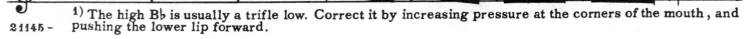

1) The high B♭ is usually a trifle low. Correct it by increasing pressure at the corners of the mouth, and pushing the lower lip forward.

26th Lesson
MISCELLANEOUS EXERCISES
(in E♭ Major)

27th Lesson
MISCELLANEOUS EXERCISES
(in A Major)

Be careful not to overblow C♯.

28th Lesson
MISCELLANEOUS EXERCISES
(in E Major)

Consult chart for fingering of C# and D#.

C× = D♮ (see p. 9)

Twenty-ninth Lesson
MISCELLANEOUS EXERCISES
(In A♭ Major)

No. 1 is the scale of A♭ major.

No. 2 is the chord of A♭ major.

No. 3 is an exercise in 4/4 time. Play staccato and very slowly at first. Study carefully and be careful not to over-blow the instrument, which is rather a common fault with beginners. Try to acquire a clear full tone, in which lies the real beauty of the instrument.

No. 4 is in 3/4 time and should be played in strict time. Do not hurry the slurred notes, but give them the same value as the staccato notes.

No. 5 is in 2/4 time. Three notes slurred and one staccato.

No. 6 is a scale exercise in 4/4 time. Take notice of the different slurrings.

No. 7 is also a scale exercise in 2/4 time, sixteenth notes. Eight notes to each bar are slurred. After this exercise has been carefully practiced, the pupil will find it easy enough to play it with one breath.

29th Lesson
MISCELLANEOUS EXERCISES
(in A♭ Major)

Thirtieth Lesson
SIXTEENTH NOTES FOLLOWED BY DOTTED EIGHTHS

This is a form of rhythm that appears very frequently, especially in Scottish Songs. It is also very characteristic of Hungarian Music. Most players perform this style of music in a jerky and disconnected manner, and it rarely sounds as it was intended to. It is in reality a sort of syncopation, and must be played with much care and considerable taste.

No. 1 is a short exercise which is intended to acquaint the pupil with this peculiar style of rhythm. The student must be careful to get the sixteenth notes precisely on the beat or count, not a second before or after. This is tremendously important. The sixteenth note must be played rather quickly and very lightly. The dotted eighth notes must be given full value. Do not emphasize the sixteenths.

No. 2 is a famous Scotch Song which almost everybody knows. It is a very pretty melody. It starts with a dotted eighth note followed by a sixteenth. The student must carefully observe each group and notice whether there is a sixteenth followed by an eighth, or vice versa. This is an important item. Smoothness of style is very essential. Give all dotted notes good value, and be sure to get the proper notes on the count.

The same rules apply to the third, fourth and fifth exercises.

30th Lesson
SIXTEENTH NOTES FOLLOWED BY DOTTED EIGHTHS

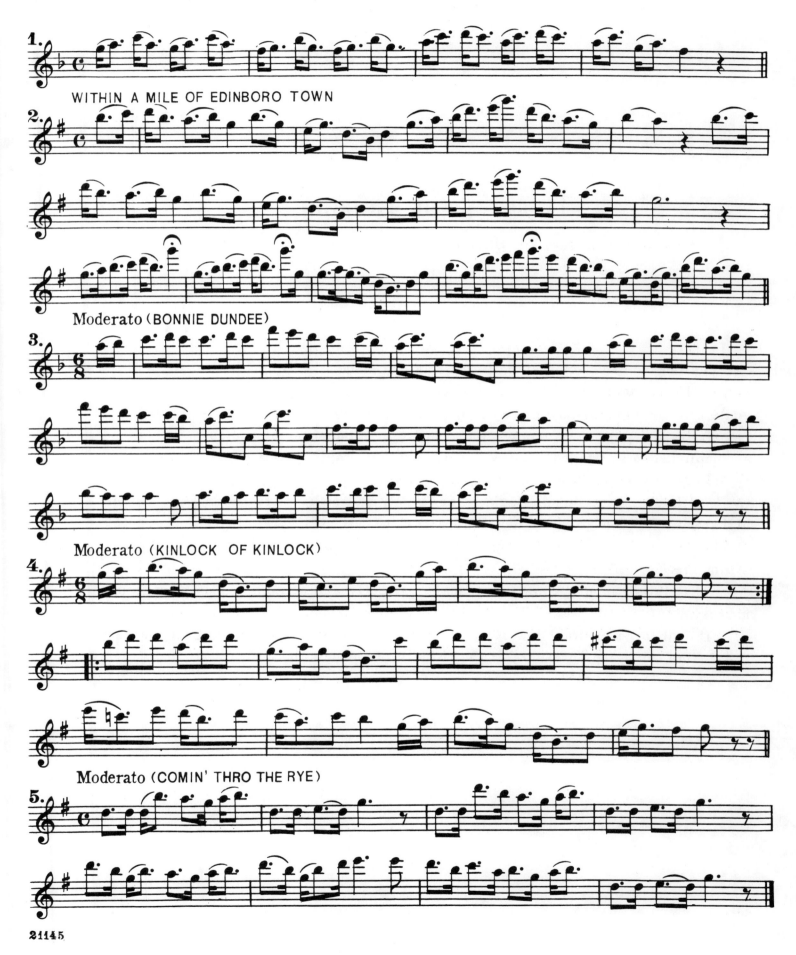

1.

WITHIN A MILE OF EDINBORO TOWN

2.

Moderato (BONNIE DUNDEE)

3.

Moderato (KINLOCK OF KINLOCK)

4.

Moderato (COMIN' THRO THE RYE)

5.

Thirty-first Lesson
SCALE STUDIES

This lesson is a scale study in the Key of C, ascending and decending, and should be conscientiously studied. It is well to remember that the playing of scales is the foundation of the technical or mechanical branch of flute playing.

After the pupil has mastered the entire major and minor scales, he will have accomplished a great deal, and will progress more rapidly as a consequence.

Play this scale slowly at first and gradually increase the speed, and see that the tone is clear and round. Begin rather softly and make a crescendo (◁) to the higher note in each group of four bars, and a decrescendo (▷) to the lowest note as marked. This is the natural manner of playing the flute as well as other wind instruments.

The flutist should know every scale perfectly and be able to play them from memory.

Do not force or over-blow the high notes. They require only slightly more breath, but sufficient pressure at the corners of the mouth.

31<u>th</u> Lesson
SCALE STUDIES

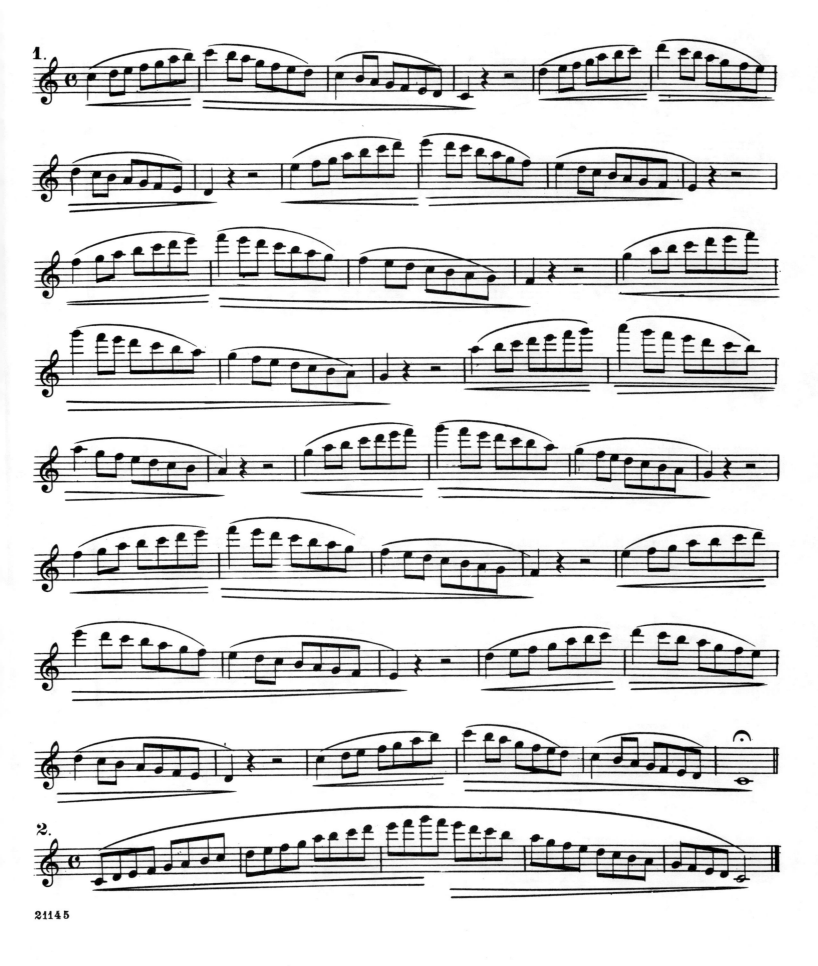

32nd Lesson
SCALE STUDIES

G (See chart for fingering of F♯ and note different fingering for the high one.)

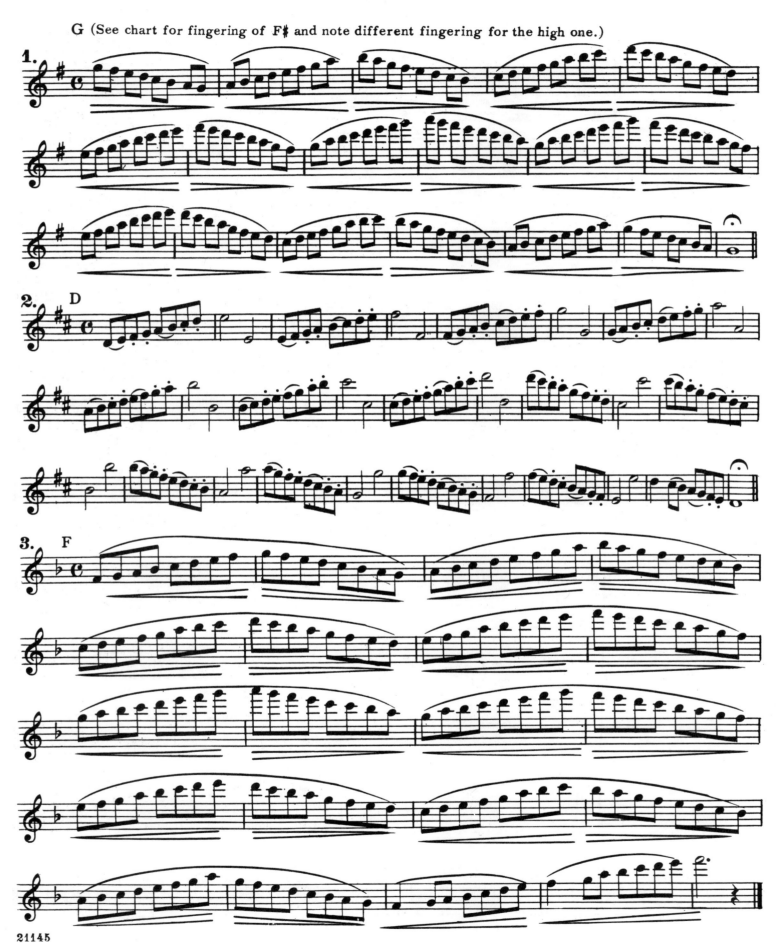

33rd Lesson
SCALE STUDIES

34th Lesson
SCALE STUDIES

35th Lesson
SCALE EXERCISES

Thirty - sixth   Lesson
TRIPLETS

When the figure "*3*" is placed over or under three notes, it denotes that they are to be played in the time of two smaller notes not so marked. Very often, however, the figure "*3*" is omitted, but it is an easy matter to figure out whether a triplet is intended or not.

The figure "*6*" placed over or under a group of notes, denotes that they are of the value of four smaller notes not so marked. This is called a double triplet.

The figures *5, 7, 9, 10* and upwards are sometimes employed under the same circumstances. These are called groups.

No. 1 is in $\frac{2}{4}$ time. The triplet comes on the first beat of each bar. Remember that each triplet must contain three even notes, and that the three notes of the triplet come on one beat. Count as indicated.

No. 2 is in $\frac{4}{4}$ time, and contains a triplet on each beat of the first three bars. Be sure to count the rests and give them their full value.

Nos. 3 and 4 are also in $\frac{4}{4}$ time and are to be played in the same manner as the preceding exercise. The time is very simple, four beats to each bar and on each beat three notes or a triplet.

No. 5 is in $\frac{2}{4}$ time. Play slowly at first counting four eighths to each bar. The first triplet on the first count, the second triplet on the second count, the third on the third count, and the eighth note on the fourth count. The three notes of the triplet have the value of an eighth. After this has been carefully studied, begin to practice it two in a bar. That would put the first two triplets on the first count and the remaining triplet and the eighth note on the second. Master the time and fingering and even tonguing.

36th Lesson
TRIPLETS

Thirty-seventh Lesson
THE CHROMATIC SCALE

No. 1 is a chromatic scale.

A chromatic scale is one that proceeds entirely by half tones. The smallest interval in music is that of a half tone.

From C to C♯ is a half tone.

From C♯ to D is a half tone.

From D to D♯ is a half tone and so on.

Listen carefully and train your ear to distinguish between a whole and a half tone. You can soon accustom your ear to the different intervals.

Play number 1 over several times and be careful of the intonation. Listen to the second C♯ and do not play it too high.

No. 2 is a chromatic scale ascending and descending. It is written in quarter notes. Study the fingering from the chart and see that the tongue and fingers work simultaneously.

Besides remembering how these chromatic scales sound, it will be beneficial to look them over carefully and try to remember how they look on paper. In fact, try to form a picture in your mind of all the music you play. This is the greatest aid in memorizing.

These chromatic exercises should be practiced very diligently.

Nos. 3 and 4 contain more chromatic scales. Chromatic scales are the easiest to remember in regard to intervals, for the progressions are all by half tones only.

Major and minor scales progress by both half and whole tones. There is no better exercise for finger technique than the chromatic scale, but, unless it is correctly practiced, no benefit can be derived.

The fingers must be quick and accurate, and must not move too quickly or too slowly, so that each note has its proper place.

After the exercises can be played smoothly at a moderate tempo, begin to play them faster.

In playing scales of all kinds rapidly, there is a great tendency to press the fingers too hard on the keys. The less pressure used, the lighter and more rapid the technique will become.

37th Lesson
THE CHROMATIC SCALE

Thirty-eighth Lesson
THE CHROMATIC SCALE

No. 1 is a slurring exercise composed of triplets. Three notes to each beat: The twelve notes in each bar are slurred. Smoothness and evenness of fingering are essential in all these exercises.

After the pupil has studied these exercises as marked (slurred), they may be practiced staccato.

No. 2 is an exercise in $\frac{6}{8}$ time. Count two beats to each bar. This exercise progresses chromatically; that is, the first note in each bar is a half tone higher than in the preceding bar. Play very slowly, as it is very difficult.

No. 3 is in $\frac{3}{4}$ time. Count three quarters to each bar. Two bars are played with one slur. After the pupil is sure of his fingering and can play these exercises without hesitancy, he should increase the speed.

Play as quickly as you can play smoothly and evenly—no quicker.

No. 4 is the entire playable register of the modern flute, chromatically arranged. It is not necessary for the pupil to practice this exercise above high Bb. It is put in here more as an example of the possiblities of the instrument.

The most important part of these exercises is to master the fingering. You must be sure of every note and not hesitate. Play these over many times each day. They help to make the lips and fingers supple.

Good players are not developed in a few months. Be satisfied if your improvement is steady. Let your progress be "slow but sure."

See next lesson for explanation regarding triplets.

38th Lesson
CHROMATIC SCALES

Thirty - ninth Lesson

EXERCISE FOR DEVELOPING TECHNIQUE IN BOTH HANDS

In the playing of any instrument, certain exercises are important for developing the fingers. These exercises, if practiced properly, will prove of great benefit to the student. Some bars will be found to be considerably easier than others. In some instances, the fingering will seem perfectly free and natural, while in other places it will seem stiff and forced. It would be wise to make a complete exercise of each bar that seems difficult. Play it over and over again. The fingers will not limber up in a day, but through systematic practice, all difficulties will eventually be overcome. In exercises such as these, the student must use discretion. Devote most of the time to the troublesome bars. The fingers must not be allowed to become stiff. Exercises of this kind, together with the scales and chromatic exercises, should be indulged in daily. While they may be monotonous to many players, it must not be lost sight of that many of the exercises that are most uninteresting to practice give the greatest amount of benefit.

39th Lesson
EXERCISES FOR DEVELOPING TECHNIQUE IN BOTH HANDS

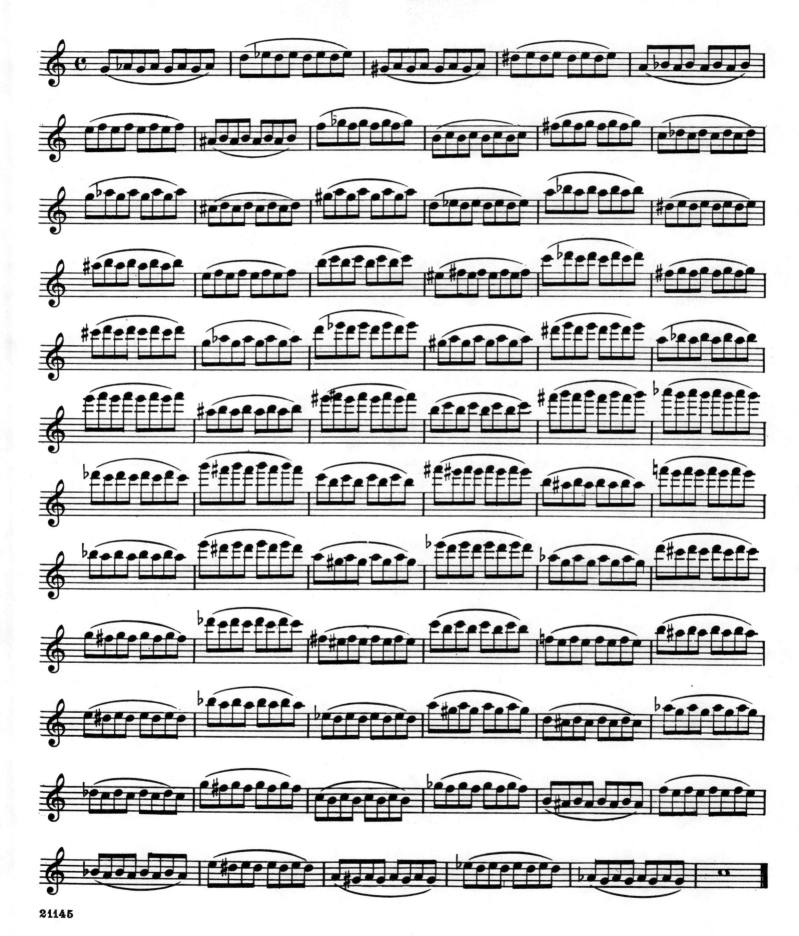

Fortieth Lesson
PREPARATORY EXERCISES ON THE GRUPETTO

The next few lessons will prove of great value in studying the Grupetto which we will take up shortly.

You will notice that there are always three notes slurred, followed by a staccato note. Play the slurred notes very evenly. Give the staccato note an accent, and separate it well from the grouped notes. Tongue it well.

Nos. 1, 2 and 3 are the same, except that they are written in different keys.

Nos. 4 and 5 are similar to the others, except that they are written in sixteenth notes.

Play very slowly at first and master the fingering. Then increase the tempo.

This form is used to a large extent in the playing of variations.

In the next lesson, the Grupetto proper will be explained.

Nos. 6 and 7 will serve to demonstrate how useful exercises of the above kind are in the playing of variations.

No. 7 is a form of variation very frequently used in flute and piccolo solos.

No. 6. This theme is used as the national air of several countries and is universally familiar to everybody. To us it is known as "America". The theme itself is most simple.

No. 7 is a variation on that theme.

A variation is one of a set or series of transformations of a theme by means of harmonic, rhythmic and melodic changes and embellishments. Play smoothly and in strict time. Do not hurry the slurred notes. Be sure to accent the notes so marked, as they indicate the theme. Always rest when you feel the least bit fatigued. If you have studied the first five exercises carefully, No. 7 will be quite easy to master.

40th Lesson
PREPARATORY EXERCISES ON THE GRUPETTO

America
THEME AND VARIATIONS

Forty-first Lesson

THE GRUPETTO

The Grupetto (or Turn) is indicated thus: (∞)

It consists of several extra or grace notes. Sometimes the notes are written in the music; at other times only designated by the sign.

The sign is placed either over or after a principal note, and consists of three grace notes, viz., that on the degree next above, then the degree of the principal note, and lastly that on the degree below, and then returning to the principal note.

Notice the first bar of Exercise No. 1.

When a sharp is placed under a Turn, as in the second bar of first Exercise, the lowest note must be made sharp.

When a flat is placed above a Turn as in the third bar, it signifies that the highest note must be made flat.

When sharps are placed above and below the Turn, it indicates that both the highest and lowest notes must be sharpened.

A flat, double flat, sharp, double sharp, or natural placed in similar positions affect the notes in like manner.

If there are no accidentals marked over or under the Turn, both the upper and lower grace notes must be played in accordance with the Key Signature.

The Grupetto should be played smoothly and gracefully.

The Grupetto may also be inverted, but in that case the notes are generally written.

In exercise No. 1, each bar contains a Grupetto with a different indication. Study this carefully. This is merely an example.

In this lesson, the upper line shows how the music is written, and the second line, how it should be played.

Play No. 2 slowly. Count four even quarters to a bar.

In order to play in strict time, it is necessary to take from the value of one of the longer notes, so as to make room for the grace notes. Therefore shorten the half note. For instance, in the first bar, count one, two, and immediately without waiting after the second count, bring in your Grupetto notes evenly but not too quickly, so that the G comes precisely on the third count and the quarter note C on the fourth.

In No. 3, play the Grupetto immediately after the first count, so that strict rhythm may be maintained.

There is no rule for the playing of Grupettos or other fancy notes. It is left to a great extent to the judgment and good taste of the performer.

It would be wise to play these exercises first without the extra notes, just as they are written on the top line; then with the extra notes.

In all the exercises of this lesson, all the notes retain their full time value, except the first note of each bar, which is shortened a trifle so that the Grupetto may be played without interfering with the time and rhythm of the other notes in the bar.

The Grupetto is very effective and graceful when well played.

Play the Grupetto as lightly as possible, as they are not principal notes, but merely ornamental.

There are other forms of the Grupetto, but it is not necessary or advisable to take them up at this time.

41 st Lesson
THE GRUPETTO OR TURN

1. as written

2. Andante
as written

3. as written

Forty-second Lesson
GRACE NOTES

There are many kinds of grace notes, some of which are explained in this lesson.

Grace notes are ornaments of melody which are implies in smaller characters, and, as their name implies, are introduced as embellishments. They do not form an essential part of the time value of the bar, but appear as a surplus, and their actual value is deducted either from the notes that they precede or follow. Grace notes are of different kinds, and are clearly defined by their designations, which comprise the Appoggiatura the Acciaccatura, the Grupetto or Turn, the Shake or Trill, the Mordente, the Portamento, and the Cadenza.

No. 1. This particular kind of grace note is called "Acciaccatura". The name is unimportant, as most embellishments are known by musicians as simply "Grace notes."

This grace note consists of a small eighth note, with a line drawn through its tail, which signifies that it must be played lightly and rapidly in order that the accent should fall on the principal note. It should be slurred to the principal note.

No. 2. should be played very lightly. Do not give the grace notes any accent. They should be barely heard. The accent goes to the note to which the grace note belongs.

Play all the notes in this exercise short, except the quarters.

No. 3 has two grace notes instead of one. The exercise is a simple one.

Count four in a bar.

The quarters that are followed by grace notes must be somewhat shortened. In other words, do not dwell on the quarter, but immediately after the first count, play the grace notes so that the note that follows comes precisely on its proper beat.

No. 4 is in six-eighth time. Play it quite slowly at first. The grace notes are somewhat different than in the previous exercise. In this exercise, there is an interval of a third between each two grace notes.

There are so many different kinds of grace notes etc. that it would be impossibe to go into detail about all of them. They should be taken up by more advanced players.

In No. 5, there are three grace notes. They must be played quickly and lightly. Since all of these notes are at the beginning of the bar, they must be played a little before the first count or beat, so that the real first note of the bar comes precisely on the first beat.

The fingering must be sure and even.

42nd Lesson

GRACE NOTES

Forty - third Lesson
THE TRILL

The Trill or Shake marked thus "*tr*" or "*tr*~~~" consists of a rapid alterna-tion of the note so marked, with the note on the next degree above it. "*tr*" is an abbreviation of the word "trill."

It is necessary to practice the trill slowly at first. Then the velocity may be increased, until the utmost rapidity has been reached.

A trill, as a rule, is ended with an appoggiatura, a turn or some other kind of grace notes, but this is always indicated by the notation.

As in the case of all wind instruments, the trills on the flute are not always perfect. The principal reason for this is that, no matter how carefully a flute is made, it is an absolute impossibility to make a perfect instrument, although the flute is admittedly the most perfect of all the wind instruments. They will always vary slightly in pitch, tone and intonation. Some trills are very easy to make and others are decidedly difficult. In looking at the chart carefully, fingerings will be found for some trills. Try to find the one best in tune on your particular flute.

No. 1 is a simple preparatory exercise in half tones. Each bar may be repeat-ed as often as the pupil chooses. In fact, each bar may be used as a separate ex-ercise. Use only the correct trill fingering, as marked in the chart.

No. 2 shows how the trill is written and how it is played. As a rule, when the trill is long it begins rather slowly and increases in speed as it progresses. This sort of trill is very effective. The intervals are half and whole tone trills.

You will notice that the trill ends with a turn or extra notes (grace notes,) which makes a very satisfactory ending. Do not play the grace notes or turn too fast.

No. 3 is a melody adorned with trills. Only trill the notes so marked and terminate the trill as designated.

The trill depends mostly on the evenness of fingering, and requires diligent practice to master.

No. 4 is also a melody containing more trills in the upper register.

Careful practice will overcome all difficulties in a short time.

43rd Lesson
THE TRILL

Forty-fourth Lesson
THE TRILL

No. 1 is an exercise containing various kinds of trills and should be played quite slowly. All should terminate as marked.   In the eighth and ninth bars will be found trills without the turn or appoggiatura and are to be played as marked. In the thirteenth bar occurs what is termed a "chain trill." Each note slurs into the other without any extra embellishments. In the nineteenth and twentieth bars will be found a chain trill written in eighth notes. Slur the two bars, but be sure to make each trill distinct.

No. 2 is an exercise in 4/4 time, containing half and whole tone trills and shakes. Look at the chart carefully before attempting to play the high trills and do not allow them to become boisterous or explosive. They are just as easy to play as the others, if practiced sufficiently.

No. 3 is an exercise in 2/4 time and should be played at a faster tempo than the previous exercises. The twelfth bar is written "legato staccato" or soft staccato. In the thirteenth and sixteenth bars, the turn may be simplified, playing the C# by closing No. 2 key with the middle finger of the right hand, at the same time keeping all the fingers down that are in use for the D.

44th Lesson
THE TRILL

Forty - fifth Lesson

MAJOR AND MINOR SCALES

In order to master any instrument, a person must know something of the rudiments of music. One may be able to play after a fashion, without having any knowledge of music, but one cannot play correctly. Many people endowed with great natural talent do not study the fundamental principles of music. This is a great mistake. To be endowed with talent is a great blessing, but in order to play musically correctly, one must understand the rudiments of music.

It is absolutely necessary to know the value of time and rhythm, to know the various scales, both Major and Minor, to know the meaning of all signs and expression marks, etc.

Instead of giving new exercises to practice for each lesson, it will be of great benefit to the student to receive a lesson here and there, that is intended to increase his general knowledge of music.

If the student has the necessary knowledge, he will know how each passage should be played, and why. Then by conscientiously practicing the necessary exercises and studies, (which is the mechanical part of the work) he cannot fail to achieve the desired result.

You will notice that these scales are arranged in groups of two. The reason for this is that each Major scale has a relative Minor scale, and the signature of both is the same.

C Major and A Minor have the same signature.

G Major and E Minor have the same signature, and so on.

But while the signatures are the same, the scales sound vastly different.

Minor scales are related to the Major scale of which their Tonic (or key-note) forms the sixth degree, and each minor scale is written under the key signature of the Major scale to which it is related.

As an example, A is the sixth degree in the scale of C; therefore the scale of A Minor is the relative of C Major and is written without key signature of sharps and flats.

E is the sixth degree of the scale of G Major, therefore E is its relative minor, and is written in the key signature of G Major, and so on, such alteration as may be necessary to any note being indicated by ♯, ♭, or ♮ when such notes occur.

The Minor scale always bears the same signature as its relative Major scale, and the difference in its intervals is made by substituting extra sharps, flats or naturals instead of writing them in the signature.

The relative Minor scale to every Major scale is found a minor third below the Major. For instance, the relative to C Major is A Minor. A is a minor third (which means a tone and a half) lower than C.

E Minor is the relative to G Major. E is a Minor third lower than G, and so on.

There are two kinds of Minor scales, Melodic and Harmonic.

The Melodic Minor Scale has two forms: When ascending, its semitones are between the second and third and the seventh and eighth degrees, but in descending, the semitones are between the sixth and fifth and the third and second degrees.

Study the illustration carefully.

With the Harmonic Minor Scale we will not go into detail. It is not used so often.

The Harmonic Minor scale has three semitones, viz: between the second and third, the fifth and sixth and the seventh and eighth degrees, whilst, between the sixth and seventh degrees it has an interval of a tone and a half (tone and semitone). The latter is called an augmented interval. The Harmonic Minor scale does not change in descending no illustration given).

Play the scales so that your ear becomes familiar with the differences of intervals etc.

Study the diagrams and you cannot fail to understand the positions of the tones and semitones.

45th Lesson
MAJOR AND MINOR SCALES WITH SHARPS

21145 -

46ᵗʰ Lesson

MAJOR AND MINOR SCALES WITH FLATS

47th Lesson
MAJOR AND MINOR CHORD EXERCISES

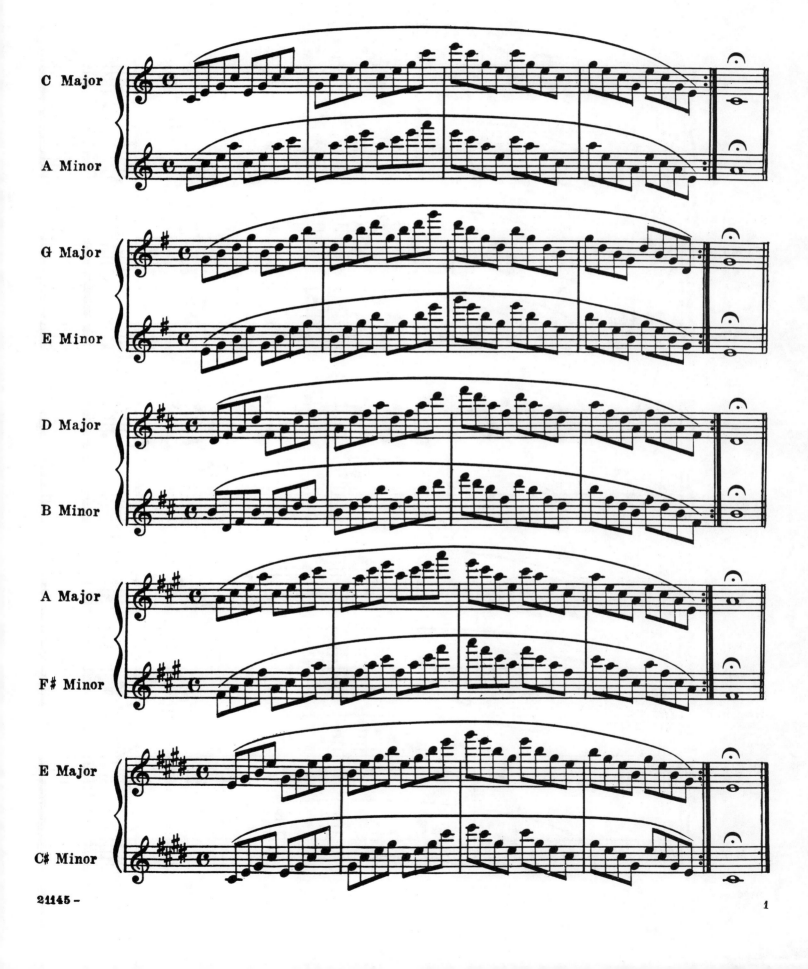

47<u>th</u> Lesson (Continued)

MAJOR AND MINOR CHORD EXERCISES

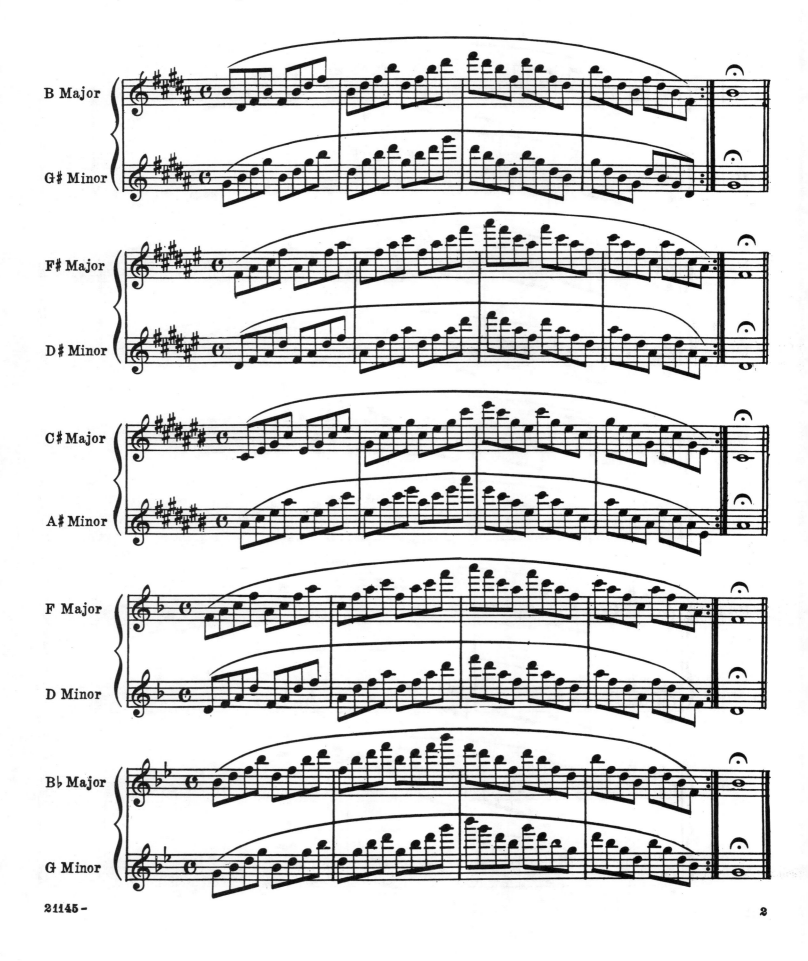

B Major

G# Minor

F# Major

D# Minor

C# Major

A# Minor

F Major

D Minor

Bb Major

G Minor

47th Lesson (Concluded)
MAJOR AND MINOR CHORD EXERCISES

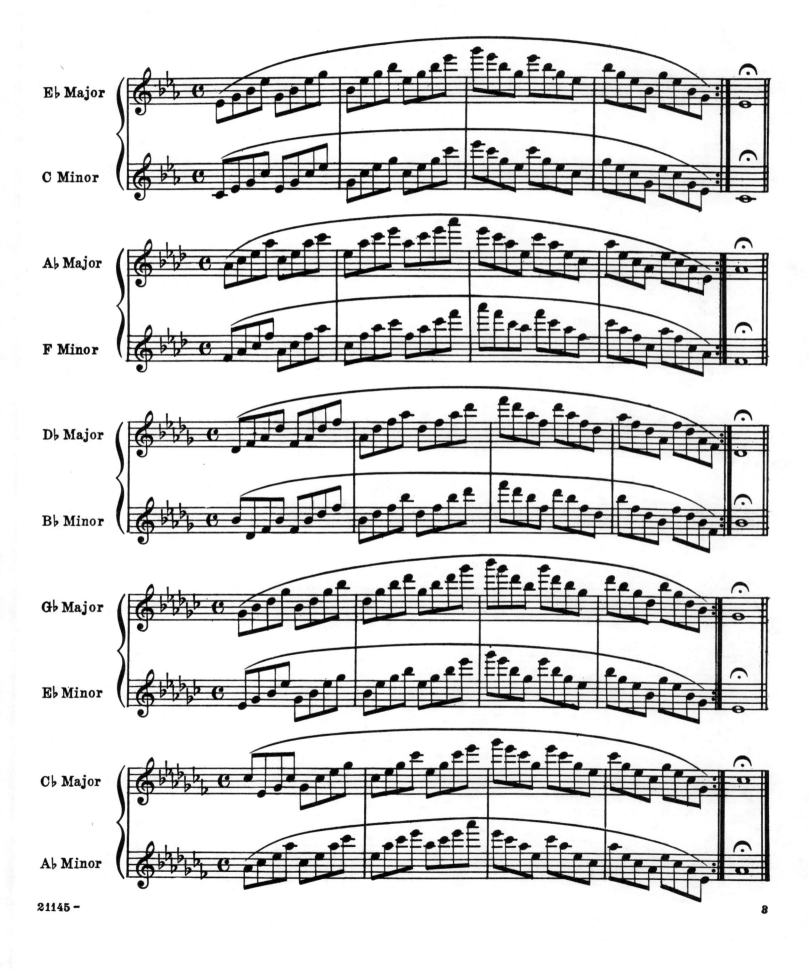

48th Lesson
MELODIC MINOR SCALES

These scales make excellent practice for finger development, tone production, and intonation
They should be practiced daily

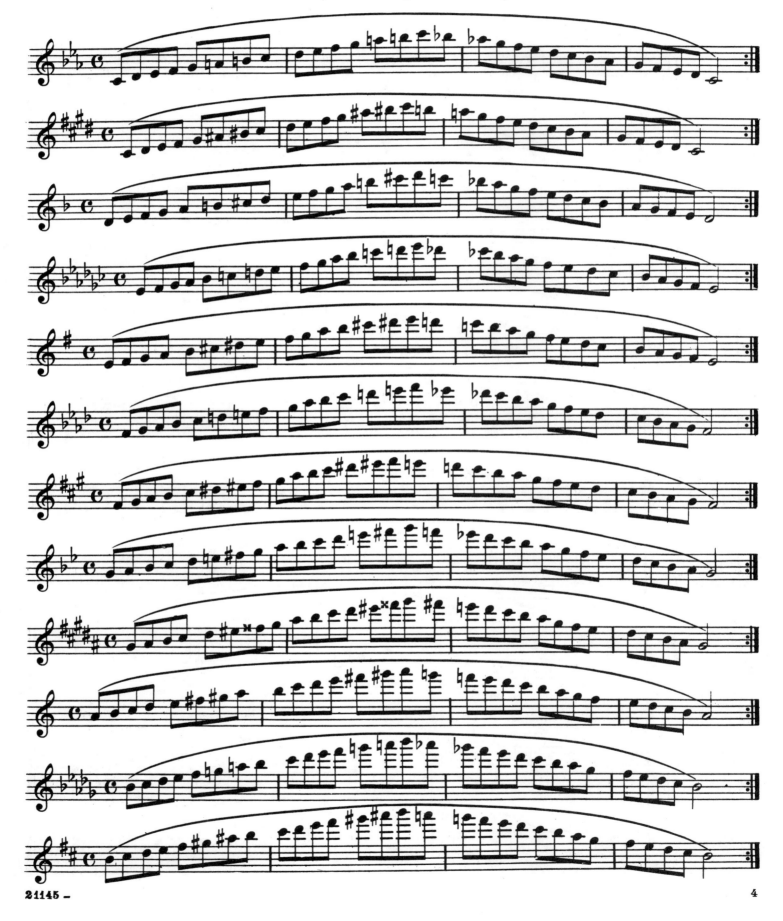

49th Lesson
HARMONIC MINOR SCALES

These scales make excellent practice for finger development, tone production and intonation.
They should be practiced daily.

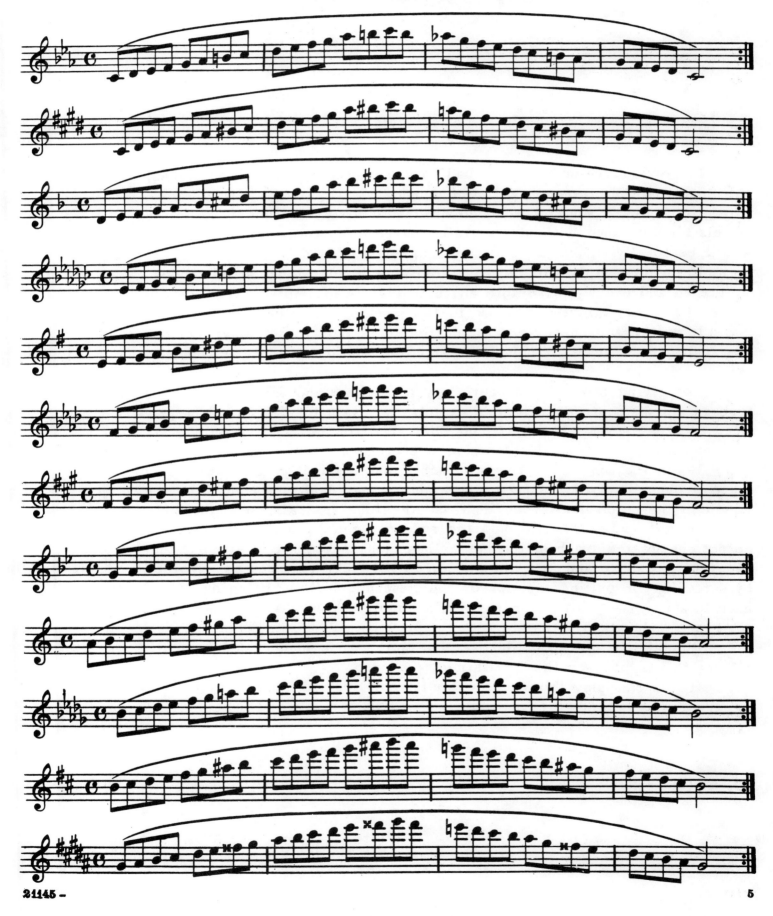

31145 —

5

Fiftieth Lesson
SUSTAINED TONES

In previous lessons, we have had various studies on sustained tones, but none with the crescendo and diminuendo.

Until now, it would have been unwise to give the student exercises of this kind, because without a certain degree of lip development, he would be totally unable to play anything of this kind.

From now on, it will be most advisable to play long, steady tones first, each and every day, before anything else is attempted. Then devote fifteen or twenty minutes or more to this sort of practice.

It will not be necessary to confine one's self to the playing of only one scale. Each scale in this book should be practised in the same manner.

For giving strength and certainty to the lips, and for improving the tone as well as controlling it, this exercise is invaluable. It should be practiced each day several times without fail. The student will soon notice the benefit derived from this and similar exercises.

Begin the tone as softly as possible, but distinctly. The tone should respond immediately it has been struck. Make a gradual crescendo till the middle of the second bar. Then decrease the tone gradually until the end.

Do not make the crescendo too suddenly, and in increasing the tone do not change the pitch of the note. In a crescendo, there is a strong tendency to get sharp and in a diminuendo to get flat. This can be avoided by spreading or pulling the lips on the crescendo and by bringing them back to a normal position on the diminuendo. In this way, the tone will become perfectly steady.

Play all the notes in this exercise in the same manner and be careful not to over-blow on the fortissimo.

If you can play this exercise well, your lips are under good control.

50th Lesson

SUSTAINED TONES

For Developing the Tone and Strengthening the Lips

21145-

Fifty-first Lesson
INTERVALS

Exerises of this kind are very important. They should be practiced with particular care. Great attention should be paid to the intonation. Nothing will do more to train the ear than exercises on the interval. The student should learn to discriminate between a second and third, or a fourth and fifth. In fact, he should know his intervals so thoroughly that he can sing the second, third, fourth, fifth, octave etc. of any given note. After he is able to do this, he should learn the difference between major and minor, diminished and augmented intervals, etc. A player of any wind instrument who does not develop his ear properly, can never hope to achieve any great success as a performer. The player, while sounding one note, should anticipate the next. In other words, he should know his intervals so well, that he hears mentally just how the next one ought to sound.

Exercise No. 1 is written in thirds. The notes are all quarters and should be played evenly.

No. 2 is in fourths and should be played in a similar manner to the first exercise.

No. 3 is in fifths. Care should be taken to connect the notes smoothly.

No. 4 is an exercise in sixths.

No. 5 is in sevenths. The greater the interval is between the two notes, the more difficult it becomes to slur them smoothly.

No. 6 is in octaves. Be very careful to play them in tune.

51st Lesson

INTERVALS

For Daily Practice

1.

2.

3.

4.

5.

6.

Fifty - second Lesson

EMBOUCHURE EXERCISES

These lessons are quite difficult, and are therefore placed toward the end of this method.

They are very valuable for making the lips flexible and for strengthening the corners of the mouth, this being essential to good flute playing.

Take one exercise and play it over and over until you can play it without breaking the slur and with good intonation.

The pupil can play Nos. 1, 3, 5, 7 and 9 and perfect them, before attempting Nos. 2, 4, 6, 8, and 10. At first, take breath as marked. After sufficient practice, increase the tempo and play each exercise in one breath.

These exercises will do much towards strengthening the lips and improving the tone. They should be practiced daily.

52nd Lesson

EMBOUCHURE EXERCISES

Fifty-third Lesson

MISCELLANEOUS TECHNICAL EXERCISES

Most of the exercises so far have been rather short. The following will be found somewhat longer and will require slightly more effort on the part of the pupil, as breath must be taken very quickly, so as not to disturb the even rhythm.

No. 1 is in $\frac{2}{4}$ time, key of G Major. Play very slowly and staccato at first, and take breath between the bars when necessary. After the tempo has been increased, breath may be taken less frequently.

No. 2 is in $\frac{3}{4}$ time, key of E♭ major. After this exercise has been thoroughly mastered (playing the B♭ with the first finger of the right hand), the pupil may practice it with the double B♭ key, using the thumb of the left hand. The low notes must be attacked the same as the higher notes.

53rd Lesson
MISCELLANEOUS TECHNICAL EXERCISES

54th Lesson
MISCELLANEOUS TECHNICAL EXERCISES

55th Lesson
MISCELLANEOUS TECHNICAL EXERCISES

Fifty - sixth Lesson
DOUBLE TONGUING

The Flute has an advantage over all other woodwind instruments in the matter of playing rapid staccato passages. While it is possible on all reed instruments to play only single tonguing, the flutist can play both double and triple tonguing, which is used to great advantage.

In the playing of double tonguing, it is possible to use several syllables: Di-ke, Tu-que, Te-ke; but I have found that the first given, Di-ke (pronounced as Dickey), is the most practical. It is less tiring than Te-ke, and with sufficient practice can be made to sound as distinct and short.

In pronouncing the syllables slowly, you will notice that the first half is produced with the tongue and the second is back in the throat, but must be made to sound as short as the first syllable.

In order to acquire even and distinct double tonguing, it is necessary to practice very slowly at first, with slightly more accent on the second syllable, as it is the weaker of the two.

Care must be taken not to press the flute too tightly against the lips, as that will make the tone hard and less vibrant, and if held too loosely will not allow of sufficient control to produce a distinct sharp staccato. A happy medium between the two will bring the best results.

Exercises from No. 1 to No. 6 inclusive are all written in quarter notes so that the pupil will begin slowly. It is a serious mistake to acquire speed at first. The slower the beginning, the more even will be the staccato.

No. 7 is written in eighth notes and should be practiced at a somewhat increased tempo, that is, after the previous exercises have been thoroughly mastered. The note changes at every bar.

No. 8 is also written in eighth notes with the note changing every third quarter of the bar.

No. 9 will be found more difficult as the note changes on each quarter of every bar. Care should be exercised to produce the low notes just as distinctly as the higher ones.

56th Lesson
DOUBLE TONGUING

Fifty-seventh Lesson
DOUBLE TONGUING

No. 1 is perhaps the easiest form found in double tonguing, two notes slurred and two staccato, there being less strain on the tongue than in continued staccato.

No. 2 begins with an up beat on the leading tone. The eighth and quarter notes are all played with single tongue stroke. Absolute rhythm is necessary to play this exercise properly.

No. 3 begins with a single tongue stroke, and the double tongue begins on the second half of the first quarter. Be sure to give the rests their full value, in order to maintain strict rhythm.

57th Lesson
DOUBLE TONGUING

Fifty-eighth Lesson
TRIPLE TONGUING

In the playing of triple tonguing, three syllables are used-the first two as in double tonguing, Di-ke, with the added syllable forming the triplet Di-ke-te. It is also possible to play triple tonguing with the double tongue syllable, but one must always be careful to bring the accent on the first note of each trip-let. Thus

The pupil should practice both ways and decide for himself which one he prefers.

Exercise No. 1 consists of only two different notes and should be practiced slowly until it can be played very evenly.

No. 2. In this exercise, the note changes on the second half of every bar, and it is absolutely essential that the tongue and fingers act simultaneously, otherwise the sense of rhythm will be lost.

No. 3 is written in 2/4 time, sixteenth notes, to give the impression of a quicker tempo.

No. 4 is written in sixteenth notes. In the first, second, fourth, sixth and eighth bars, the eighth note has the value of one triplet and should be played with the syllable Te.

No. 5 is written in the lower register of the flute and will require more practice than exercises in the higher registers. The dotted quarter has the value of three triplets, and the quarter without the dot the value of two triplets.

58th Lesson
TRIPLE TONGUING

Fifty - ninth Lesson
CADENZAS

Most instrumental solos in the larger forms contain one or two ca -
denzas, and often three. Many of the well-known operatic arias and other
vocal numbers also have cadenzas. In some instances, these cadenzas have
really made the arias famous. Instrumental cadenzas for the flute appear
so frequently that they become a very important item to soloists, as well
as those who occupy the first positions in our orchestras and bands.
As a general thing, cadenzas are rather difficult, and often extremely so, but
this is not always the case. Orchestra and band players frequently become
alarmed when they are confronted with a piece that contains a cadenza, because a cadenza is always a solo and must therefore be played alone. Soloists, on the contrary, lay a great deal of importance upon these passages,
and often when selecting new music will look first at the cadenza to see if
it is effective and elaborate enough.

When a cadenza (or cadence) is found, it indicates that the measure
of time is suspended, and its performance left to the pleasure and judg -
ment of the player. It should be played tastefully and as a rule, in corre-
spondence with the general character of the composition. There is absolutely no rule for the playing of cadenzas, and it is left entirely to the taste and
discretion of the performer. Very often cadenzas are written simply to show
the range of the instrument, and the technical capabilities of the performer. In
many instances, soloists change the cadenzas in order to display their own
strong points. They even insert entire new cadenzas at times. Very often
the composer leaves it to the performer to use his own cadenzas, so that he
can display to the best advantage his capabilities as a performer. It is
much easier to render effectively music which has to be played in a certain
designated and strict time, such as $\frac{4}{4}$, $\frac{6}{8}$, $\frac{3}{4}$, etc. But in cadenzas, where
the regular time is dispensed with, it requires considerable taste and skill
to make them sound artistic and impressive. Cadenzas are often very long,
and the more extensive they are the more difficult it becomes to render them
so as to keep up the interest and hold the attention of the auditors. In play -
ing together with other instruments, many little defects can be concealed, but
in a cadenza, which is absolutely free, open and unaccompanied, the performer must rely on a faultless rendition to be successful.

Many of the most famous operatic, as well as other cadenzas, are
written for voice and flute. The famous cadenza from the "Mad Scene" in
"Lucia di Lammermoor" is one of the numerous cadenzas for Soprano and
Flute.

59th Lesson
CADENZAS

Collection of Songs and Solos

FOLK SONG

1.

EVENING SONG

2.

HOW CAN I LEAVE THEE?

3.

O SANCTISSIMA

4.

NEARER MY GOD TO THEE

5.

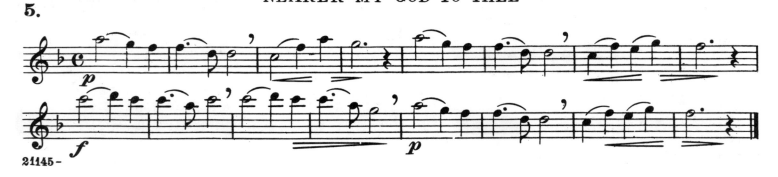

21145-

SILENT NIGHT, HOLY NIGHT

6.

BELIEVE ME IF ALL THOSE ENDEARING YOUNG CHARMS

7.

DRINK TO ME ONLY WITH THINE EYES

8.

MY OLD KENTUCKY HOME

9.

21145

AULD LANG SYNE

10.

Scotch

LOVES OLD SWEET SONG

11.

Molloy

LAST ROSE OF SUMMER

12.

Irish

LOCH LOMOND

13.

Old Scotch

BERCEUSE FROM "JOCELYN"

14.

B. Godard

15.

TRÄUMEREI

R. Schumann

21145

TURKISH MARCH

16. Allegro moderato

Beethoven

WILD ROSE

17. Andante

Terschak

PASTORALE
(SHEPHERD'S SONG)

18.

Goetzl

LARGO

19.

Handel

LE CYGNE
(THE SWAN)

20.

C. Saint-Saëns

THE RED SARAFAN

21.

Russian Ballad

SERENADE

22.

Jos. Haydn

SPRING SONG

23.

Felix Mendelssohn

Allegretto grazioso

CAVATINA

J. Raff

24. Larghetto quasi Andante

INTERMEZZO SINFONICO
from
CAVALLERIA RUSTICANA

Pietro Mascagni

25. Andante sostenuto (♩ = 54)

Etude I
THE BROOK

Allegro moderato

Ernest F. Wagner

Etude II
TARANTELLE

Ernest F. Wagner

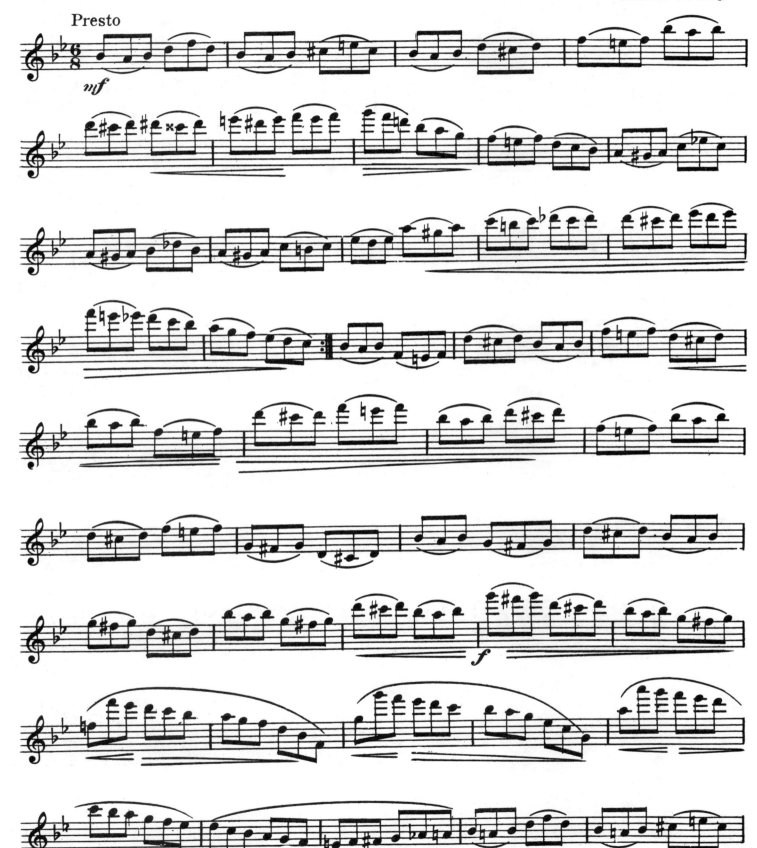

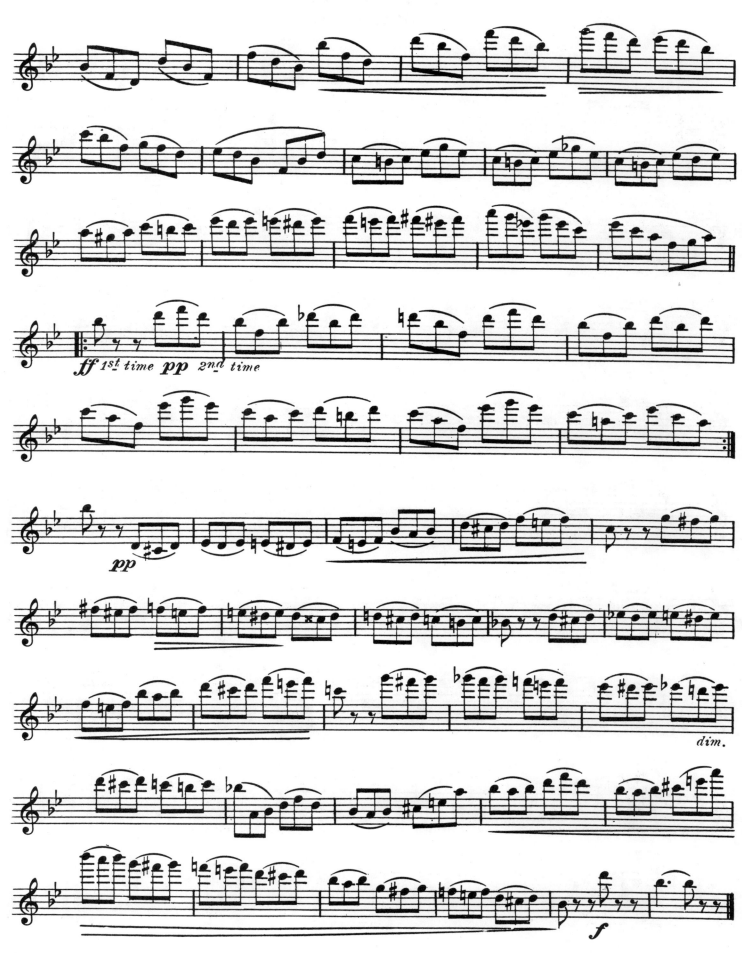

Etude II

Etude III
SYMPHONIC

Ernest F. Wagner

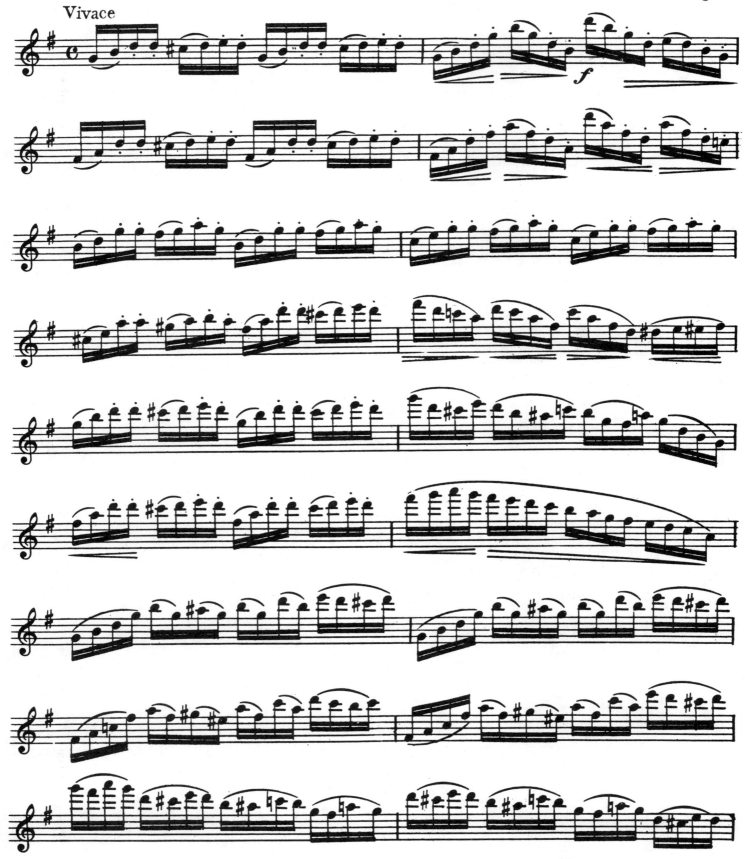

Etude IV
BRILLANTE

Ernest F. Wagner

Etude V
FANTASTIQUE

Ernest F. Wagner

Etude VI
STACCATO

Ernest F. Wagner

Moderato assai

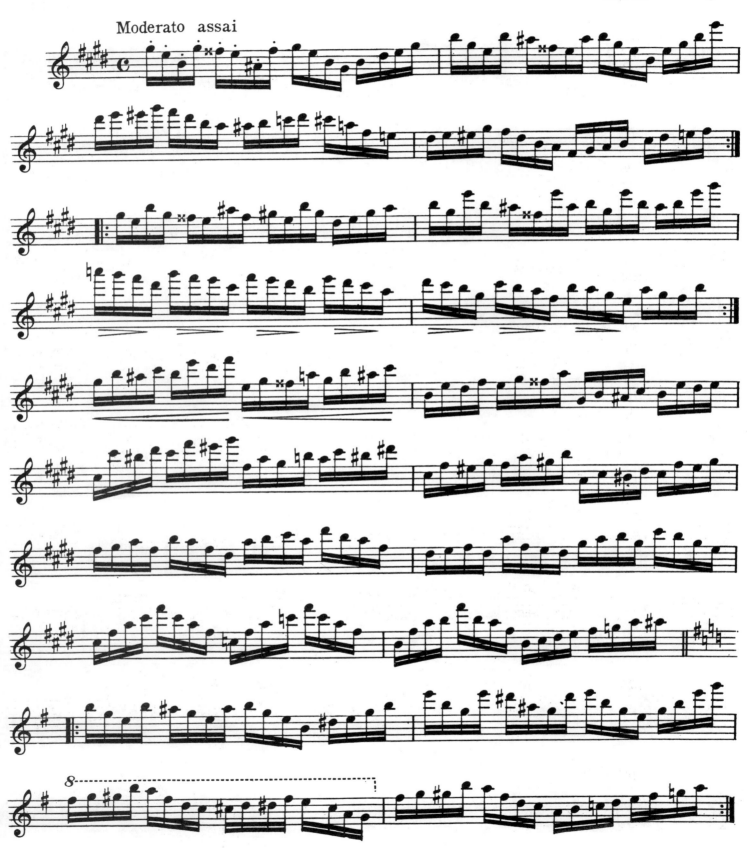

Etude VII
CHROMATIC

Ernest F. Wagner

Allegro moderato

Grand Fantasie
THEME AND VARIATIONS
Aloha Oe
(Farewell to thee) Hawaiian Song

Ernest F. Wagner

Theme
Andante moderato

2nd Variation

3rd Variation

Finale

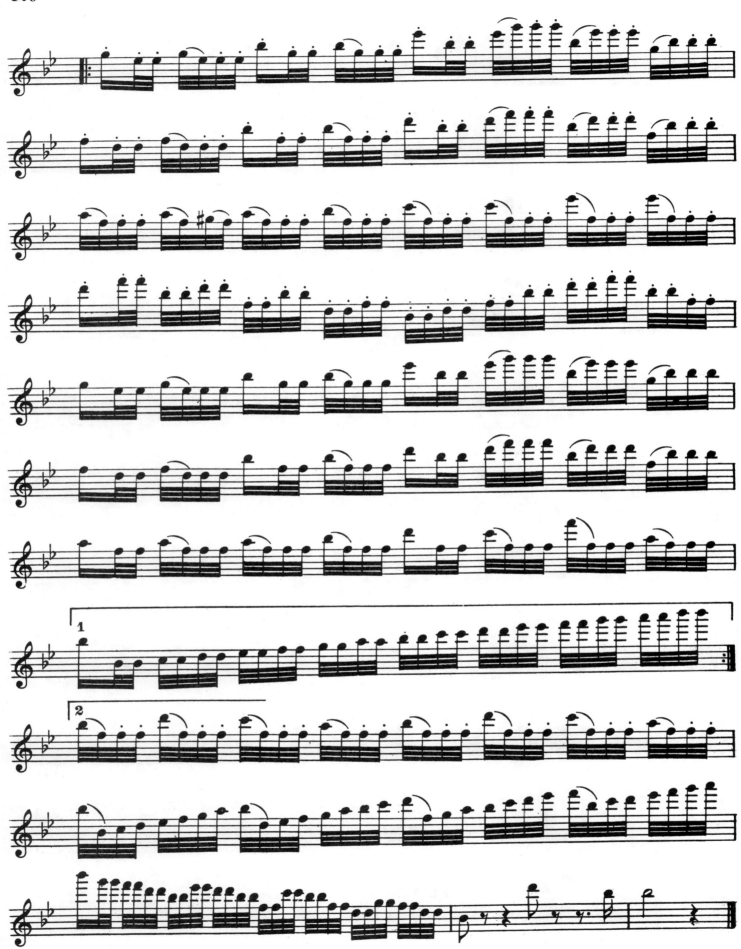